MASTERING
THE SALES LOT

Strategies to Close Deals and Maximize Profits in Any Marketplace

JAMES D JOHN

© 2024 JAMES D JOHN

All rights reserved.

No part of this book may be reproduced, stored in a retrieval system, or transmitted in any form or by any means, electronic, mechanical, photocopying, recording, or otherwise, without the prior written permission of the author, except for brief quotations used in critical reviews or articles.

Disclaimer

This book is intended for informational purposes only. The information contained herein is based on the author's research, analysis, and interpretation of available data at the time of publication. While every effort has been made to ensure the accuracy of the content, the author, publisher, and any associated entities make no guarantees about the accuracy, completeness, or suitability of the information for any particular purpose.

Table of Contents

Introduction 7

Chapter 1: 9

Understanding the Dynamics of a Sales Lot 9

    The Role of First Impressions in Sales Success 11

    Common Misconceptions and Mistakes on the Sales Lot 12

Chapter 2: 15

The Psychology of the Buyer 15

    Identifying Customer Needs and Motivations 15

    Building Trust and Rapport Quickly 16

    Recognizing and Overcoming Buyer Resistance 18

Chapter 3: 20

The Power of First Contact 20

    The Importance of Greetings and Introductions 20

    Effective Icebreakers for Any Sales Scenario 21

    Navigating Different Customer Personalities 23

Chapter 4: 27

Product Knowledge: Your Greatest Weapon 27
   Why In-Depth Knowledge Builds Credibility 27
      How to Present Product Features as Solutions 28
      Tailoring Product Pitches to Customer Needs 30
      The Role of Continuous Learning 32
      Common Pitfalls to Avoid 33

Chapter 5: 35

Mastering the Art of Persuasion 35
      Proven Persuasion Techniques for Sales Success 35
      How to Handle Objections Effectively 38
      Turning "No" into "Yes" Without Pressure 40
      The Ethics of Persuasion 42

Chapter 6: 44

Closing the Deal with Confidence 44
      Recognizing the Right Moment to Close 44
      Techniques for Seamless Deal Closures 46
      Handling Last-Minute Buyer Hesitations 48
      The Importance of Confidence in Closing 51
      Learning from Missed Opportunities 51

Chapter 7: 53

Post-Sale Strategies: Building Lifetime Customers 53

The Power of Follow-Up and After-Sales Service............53
Encouraging Repeat Business and Referrals...................55
Maintaining Long-Term Customer Relationships 57
Leveraging Technology for Post-Sale Strategies...........60
Common Pitfalls to Avoid in Post-Sale Engagement....61

Chapter 8: 64
Sales Lot Etiquette and Professionalism 64
Best Practices for Sales Professionals 64
The Role of Honesty and Transparency in Sales...............67
Maintaining Professionalism under Pressure 69
Professional Communication Skills 71
Building a Professional Reputation..72
Ethical Sales Practices..73
Leading by Example...74

Chapter 9: 76
Metrics That Matter: Measuring Success on the Sales Lot
..76
Key Performance Indicators (KPIs) for Salespeople 76
Continuous Improvement Strategies 81
Leveraging Technology for Sales Metrics.......................84
Avoiding Common Pitfalls in Sales Metrics.....................86

Chapter 10:...88

The Future of Sales Lots: Adapting to Change 88
    How Technology is Transforming Sales Lots 88
    Staying Competitive in an Evolving Sales Landscape 91
    Preparing for the Next Generation of Sales Professionals 93
    Emerging Trends in Sales Lots 95
    Challenges in Adapting to Change 97
    The Road Ahead 98
Conclusion 100

Introduction

In today's rapidly changing business environment, sales lots remain a critical hub for customer interactions, product demonstrations, and successful transactions. However, the traditional sales lot model is undergoing significant transformation, driven by advancements in technology, evolving customer expectations, and shifting market dynamics. To stay competitive, sales professionals must not only adapt to these changes but also anticipate future trends and challenges.

This book serves as a comprehensive guide for sales professionals, managers, and business owners who want to excel in the modern sales landscape. Each chapter delves into essential aspects of sales lot operations, offering actionable insights, proven strategies, and real-world examples to help professionals maximize their potential.

From mastering first impressions to leveraging advanced sales metrics, and from understanding buyer psychology to embracing future technologies, this book covers it all. You'll learn how to build lasting customer relationships, optimize sales techniques, and stay ahead of the curve in an ever-evolving industry.

Whether you're a seasoned sales veteran or just stepping into the world of sales lots, this guide will equip you with the tools, knowledge, and mindset needed to thrive. Get ready to transform your sales approach, exceed your targets, and create unparalleled value for your customers and your organization.

Chapter 1:

Understanding the Dynamics of a Sales Lot

The sales lot is more than just a physical space where transactions occur; it is an ecosystem driven by psychology, strategy, and human interaction. Whether it's an automotive dealership, a real estate site, or a retail warehouse, the sales lot operates as a dynamic environment where every element contributes to the success or failure of a sale.

At its core, a sales lot is a meeting point between buyers and sellers, but it is also a stage. The layout, the positioning of products, the demeanor of salespeople, and even the background music play significant roles in influencing customer behavior. Understanding these dynamics requires sales professionals to become adept at reading both the physical and emotional cues present on the lot.

One key dynamic is the concept of territory. Salespeople often treat the sales lot as their domain, and they must balance assertiveness with approachability. A pushy salesperson can alienate customers, while an overly passive one may miss opportunities. Another critical factor is time. Customers on a sales lot are often on a ticking clock—they want information quickly, but they also don't want to feel rushed. Striking the right balance is essential.

Furthermore, there are invisible dynamics at play, such as customer expectations and preconceived notions. A customer arriving on a sales lot may have already done extensive online research. They might know the specifications, prices, and even the sales tactics they expect to encounter. Sales professionals must be prepared to address these expectations while maintaining control of the sales process.

In short, understanding the dynamics of a sales lot means recognizing that every interaction is part of a larger choreography—one that blends psychology, timing, and effective communication.

The Role of First Impressions in Sales Success

First impressions are powerful, and in sales, they can be the deciding factor in whether a customer stays engaged or walks away. Research indicates that people form first impressions within the first seven seconds of meeting someone. On a sales lot, this fleeting moment can determine whether a potential sale moves forward or stalls out.

The first impression begins before a word is even spoken. It starts with body language, facial expressions, and overall presentation. A salesperson's attire, grooming, and posture all communicate volumes before the first word is uttered. Equally important is eye contact, which signals confidence and attentiveness.

The greeting itself is a crucial moment. A warm smile and a confident, friendly greeting can put customers at ease. Simple phrases like, *"Welcome! How can I assist you today?"* can set a positive tone. Conversely, an insincere or overly aggressive greeting can create an invisible wall between the salesperson and the customer.

Additionally, first impressions are not limited to face-to-face interaction. The layout of the sales lot, the cleanliness of the environment, and even the signage all contribute to the customer's initial feelings about the space. A cluttered or disorganized lot can create a sense of distrust, while a well-maintained and professional-looking lot instills confidence.

Salespeople should also remember that first impressions are not one-sided. Customers also present their own first impressions, and skilled sales professionals can pick up on subtle cues—body language, tone of voice, and choice of words—to gauge customer intent and mood.

In the end, first impressions are not about perfection; they are about establishing trust, respect, and approachability within those crucial opening seconds.

Common Misconceptions and Mistakes on the Sales Lot

Success on a sales lot is often hindered by common misconceptions and mistakes that both new and experienced salespeople fall into. Recognizing these pitfalls is the first step toward avoiding them and improving overall sales performance.

1. The Hard Sell Always Works: One of the biggest misconceptions is that aggressive, high-pressure tactics are the most effective way to close a deal. While they might yield short-term results, these tactics often lead to buyer remorse, negative reviews, and lost repeat business. Modern customers value transparency and trust over pressure.

2. Every Customer is Ready to Buy: Another mistake is assuming that every customer walking onto the sales lot is ready to make a purchase. Many customers are in the research or decision-making phase, and pushing them too hard can drive them away.

3. Talking More Means Selling More: Sales professionals sometimes believe that the more they talk, the more likely they are to close a deal. However, active listening is often more powerful than an uninterrupted sales pitch. Listening allows salespeople to understand customer needs and tailor their approach accordingly.

4. Ignoring Follow-Ups: Many salespeople make the mistake of viewing the sale as the end of the relationship. In reality, post-sale follow-ups can lead to repeat business, referrals, and stronger customer loyalty.

5. Underestimating Non-Verbal Communication: Salespeople often focus so much on their pitch that they neglect non-verbal signals. Poor eye contact, closed-off body language, or even an overly distracted demeanor can sabotage a sale.

6. Failure to Adapt to Different Customer Types: Every customer is unique, yet many salespeople use the same approach for everyone. Successful sales professionals adapt their style to fit the customer's personality, preferences, and buying behavior.

7. Lack of Product Knowledge: Nothing undermines credibility faster than a salesperson who can't answer basic questions about their product. Sales professionals must be experts in what they're selling, able to answer questions confidently and accurately.

The sales lot is an ever-changing environment where success depends on preparation, adaptability, and a keen understanding of human behavior. By mastering the dynamics of the sales lot, perfecting first impressions, and avoiding common pitfalls, sales professionals can set themselves up for consistent success. In the following chapters, we will dive deeper into specific strategies and techniques that will equip you to excel in every interaction on the sales lot.

Chapter 2:

The Psychology of the Buyer

Identifying Customer Needs and Motivations

Understanding the psychology of the buyer begins with identifying their needs and motivations. Every customer who steps onto a sales lot is driven by a mix of rational and emotional factors. These motivations may include practicality, status, fear of missing out, or even sheer impulse. A successful salesperson knows how to uncover these underlying drivers through careful observation, active listening, and asking the right questions.

One of the most effective techniques is open-ended questioning. Instead of asking, *"Are you looking for something specific today?"* which may clicit a short yes or no answer, a better question would be, *"What are you hoping to find today, and how can I help?"* This invites the customer to share their needs and expectations in more detail.

Salespeople must also pay attention to non-verbal cues. A customer's body language, tone of voice, and facial expressions can reveal a lot about their mindset. Are they relaxed and confident, or do they seem hesitant and guarded? Are their eyes drawn to a particular product, or are they distracted by something else?

Empathy is a powerful tool in identifying customer needs. Salespeople should strive to put themselves in the customer's shoes and understand their concerns and desires. When customers feel understood, they are more likely to trust the salesperson and share their true motivations.

Building Trust and Rapport Quickly

Trust is the foundation of every successful sales interaction. Without it, even the best product pitch or pricing strategy will fall flat. Building trust and rapport quickly is an essential skill that every salesperson must master.

One of the quickest ways to build trust is by being genuinely interested in the customer. People can sense insincerity, and any attempt to fake interest will usually backfire. Sales professionals should approach every interaction with curiosity and a desire to help.

Another important factor is consistency. From the initial greeting to product demonstrations and final negotiations, salespeople must ensure their words and actions align. Any inconsistency can raise red flags for customers and erode trust.

Active listening also plays a crucial role in building rapport. Customers want to feel heard and valued. When a salesperson listens carefully, repeats key points, and responds thoughtfully, it signals to the customer that their needs are a priority.

Mirroring is another effective rapport-building technique. Subtly matching the customer's body language, tone of voice, and speech patterns can create a subconscious sense of connection and comfort.

Finally, transparency is key. If there are limitations or downsides to a product, it's better to address them honestly rather than attempting to gloss over them. Customers appreciate honesty, and it builds long-term trust.

Recognizing and Overcoming Buyer Resistance

Resistance is a natural part of the sales process. Even customers who are genuinely interested in a product may experience hesitation or doubt. Successful salespeople understand that resistance isn't a dead end—it's an opportunity to address concerns and guide the customer toward a decision.

The first step in overcoming resistance is identifying its root cause. Common sources of resistance include price concerns, fear of commitment, lack of trust, or simply needing more time to decide.

Salespeople must remain calm and patient when encountering resistance. Aggressive or defensive reactions will only reinforce the customer's hesitation. Instead, sales professionals should acknowledge the customer's concerns and ask clarifying questions, such as, *"I understand that price is a concern. Is there something specific about the pricing you'd like me to explain?"*

Reframing objections can also be an effective strategy. For example, if a customer says, *"This is too expensive,"* the salesperson could respond with, *"I understand it's an investment, but let me show you how this product provides long-term value and savings."*

Another technique is the 'Feel-Felt-Found' approach: *"I understand how you feel. Other customers have felt the same way at first, but what they found was..."* This method validates the customer's concerns while gently guiding them toward a resolution.

Sometimes, resistance is simply a signal that the customer isn't ready to make a decision yet. In these cases, it's important to leave the door open for future interactions. A follow-up call or email can often reignite interest after the customer has had time to process the information.

The psychology of the buyer is a complex and fascinating aspect of sales. By identifying customer needs and motivations, building trust and rapport quickly, and recognizing and overcoming resistance, sales professionals can navigate the psychological landscape of the sales lot with confidence and success. In the next chapter, we'll explore the art of first contact and how it sets the stage for every successful sale.

Chapter 3:

The Power of First Contact

The Importance of Greetings and Introductions

The first interaction between a salesperson and a customer sets the stage for the entire sales process. A strong greeting and introduction can establish trust, create a positive atmosphere, and open the door for meaningful communication. Conversely, a poor greeting can create barriers that are difficult to overcome.

A warm, confident, and professional greeting is essential. It's not just about saying hello; it's about making the customer feel valued and welcomed. The tone of voice, facial expressions, and body language all play critical roles in this moment. A smile, firm handshake, and a genuine introduction can immediately ease tension and set a cooperative tone.

Sales professionals should aim to personalize their greetings whenever possible. For example, instead of a generic *"Can I help you?"* a better approach might be, *"Welcome to our store! I'm [Your Name], and I'm here to help you find exactly what you need today."* This conveys both enthusiasm and readiness to assist.

Introductions should also include a brief statement of purpose. This helps set expectations and assures the customer that they are in good hands. For example, *"I want to make sure you have all the information you need to make the best decision today."* Such statements signal transparency and customer focus.

Effective Icebreakers for Any Sales Scenario

After the initial greeting, the next challenge is breaking the ice. Icebreakers are small conversational tools used to ease tension, build rapport, and transition smoothly into the sales discussion.

Effective icebreakers are relevant, engaging, and customer-focused. They often involve casual, open-ended questions designed to get customers talking. For example:

- *"Is this your first time visiting us, or have you been here before?"*
- *"What brings you in today? Anything specific you had in mind?"*
- *"How has your day been so far?"*

The goal of an icebreaker is to create a natural flow of conversation without overwhelming the customer. Humor can sometimes be an effective tool, but it must be used carefully and in alignment with the customer's personality and comfort level.

Observation-based icebreakers are also highly effective. Commenting on something the customer is wearing, a product they are looking at, or even the weather can create an easy entry point for further conversation.

For example:

- *"That's a great choice you're looking at. What caught your eye about it?"*
- *"It's a beautiful day out there today, isn't it?"*

The key to a successful icebreaker is authenticity. Customers can quickly detect scripted or insincere attempts at conversation. A genuine interest in the customer's needs and experience goes a long way in building rapport.

Navigating Different Customer Personalities

No two customers are exactly alike, and successful salespeople must be adept at identifying and adapting to different customer personalities. Recognizing these personalities early in the interaction allows sales professionals to tailor their approach and communication style effectively.

1. The Decisive Buyer:

These customers are confident, goal-oriented, and usually know exactly what they want. They appreciate efficiency and straightforward information.

- **Best Approach:** Be direct, provide clear answers, and avoid unnecessary small talk.
- **Pitfall to Avoid:** Don't overwhelm them with excessive details or prolonged discussions.

2. The Analytical Buyer:

Analytical customers focus on details, data, and comparisons. They ask a lot of questions and take their time to make decisions.

- **Best Approach:** Provide thorough explanations, highlight key features, and be patient.
- **Pitfall to Avoid:** Don't rush them or dismiss their need for more information.

3. The Social Buyer:

These customers value relationships and enjoy conversation. They are often influenced by emotions and the connection they feel with the salesperson.

- **Best Approach:** Build rapport, share stories, and create a friendly, warm interaction.
- **Pitfall to Avoid:** Don't focus solely on facts and figures; emotional connection matters here.

4. The Skeptical Buyer:

These customers are cautious and may be hesitant to trust salespeople. They are likely to question motives and need reassurance.

- **Best Approach:** Be transparent, address concerns directly, and avoid overly aggressive tactics.
- **Pitfall to Avoid:** Don't dismiss their concerns or appear insincere.

5. The Indecisive Buyer:

These customers struggle to make decisions and may go back and forth on their choices.

- **Best Approach:** Guide them gently, provide reassurance, and help simplify their options.
- **Pitfall to Avoid:** Don't pressure them or make them feel rushed.

A skilled salesperson knows how to adjust their communication style and approach based on these personality types. Flexibility and keen observation are essential tools in navigating these diverse customer profiles.

The power of first contact cannot be overstated. A strong greeting, an effective icebreaker, and the ability to navigate different customer personalities are critical elements of successful sales interactions. These skills lay the foundation for trust, rapport, and productive communication, setting the stage for the rest of the sales process. In the next chapter, we will explore the importance of product knowledge and how it can enhance credibility and customer confidence.

Chapter 4:

Product Knowledge: Your Greatest Weapon

Why In-Depth Knowledge Builds Credibility

In the world of sales, credibility is everything. Without it, even the most persuasive salesperson will struggle to close deals. In-depth product knowledge is one of the most powerful tools for building and maintaining credibility with customers. When a salesperson demonstrates expertise, it reassures the customer that they are dealing with a professional who can be trusted.

Customers expect salespeople to know the products they're selling inside and out. This includes technical specifications, features, benefits, potential limitations, and even comparisons with competitor products. When a customer asks a question, they expect a prompt and confident answer. Hesitation or vague responses can immediately erode trust.

Beyond answering questions, product knowledge allows salespeople to anticipate customer concerns and address them proactively. For instance, if a customer is purchasing a high-end appliance and expresses concerns about energy consumption, a well-informed salesperson can immediately highlight energy-saving features and provide supporting data.

Moreover, deep product knowledge positions the salesperson as an advisor rather than just a seller. Customers are more likely to trust someone who offers valuable insights and helps them make informed decisions, rather than someone who simply pushes a product. In this way, knowledge shifts the salesperson from being seen as a transactional intermediary to a reliable consultant.

How to Present Product Features as Solutions

Understanding product features is one thing; presenting them as solutions to customer needs is another. The key to effective selling lies in bridging the gap between what the product offers and what the customer values.

Customers don't buy products for their features; they buy them for the outcomes those features provide. For example, someone doesn't buy a high-speed internet package because of its download speed—they buy it because they want uninterrupted streaming, fast work-from-home connections, or seamless online gaming.

To present features as solutions, salespeople must follow these key steps:

1. **Identify Customer Pain Points:** Through active listening and strategic questioning, identify what challenges or needs the customer is trying to address.
2. **Link Features to Benefits:** For each identified need, highlight a feature of the product and explain how it solves that specific problem.
3. **Use Real-World Examples:** Share success stories or anecdotes from previous customers who benefited from the same feature.
4. **Focus on Outcomes:** Instead of saying, *"This smartphone has a 48MP camera,"* say, *"With this 48MP camera, your photos will look professional, even in low light."*

The best product presentations are customer-centric. They focus less on the technical jargon and more on how the product enhances the customer's experience or resolves their specific concerns.

Tailoring Product Pitches to Customer Needs

Every customer is unique, and a one-size-fits-all sales pitch rarely works. Tailoring a product pitch means aligning your presentation with the customer's specific needs, preferences, and motivations.

1. Know Your Customer

Before tailoring a pitch, it's essential to understand the customer. Ask open-ended questions, listen actively, and observe non-verbal cues. Key details to uncover include:

- Why are they interested in the product?
- What problem are they trying to solve?
- What concerns or reservations do they have?

2. Speak Their Language

Once you have a clear understanding of the customer's needs, adjust your language and approach accordingly. For a tech-savvy customer, you might delve into detailed specifications, while for someone less familiar with the product, you'd focus more on benefits and simplicity.

For example:

- **Tech-Savvy Customer:** *"This laptop has an Intel i7 processor and 16GB of RAM, ensuring seamless multitasking even with resource-heavy software."*
- **Non-Tech-Savvy Customer:** *"This laptop is super fast and can handle multiple tasks at once without slowing down."*

3. Prioritize Key Features

Not every feature will be relevant to every customer. Highlight the features that directly address their needs and avoid overwhelming them with unnecessary information. For instance, if a customer is buying a car primarily for fuel efficiency, focus on the vehicle's mileage rather than its entertainment system.

4. Use Demonstrations and Visuals

Whenever possible, use live demonstrations or visual aids to reinforce your pitch. Let customers experience the product firsthand. For example, if selling a smart home device, show them how easy it is to control with voice commands.

5. Handle Objections Proactively

Anticipate potential objections and address them before the customer brings them up. If a customer seems hesitant about price, demonstrate the long-term value and benefits of the product.

The Role of Continuous Learning

Product knowledge isn't static. Products evolve, new features are introduced, and competitors enter the market. Salespeople must commit to continuous learning to stay informed and relevant.

- **Attend Training Sessions:** Regularly participate in product training sessions offered by your company.
- **Use the Product Yourself:** Firsthand experience provides deeper insight and confidence.

- **Study Competitors:** Understand how your product compares to similar offerings in the market.
- **Stay Updated:** Follow product updates, read manuals, and engage with internal product experts.

Sales professionals who invest in continuous learning not only improve their credibility but also set themselves apart as true experts in their field.

Common Pitfalls to Avoid

While product knowledge is essential, there are common pitfalls that salespeople must be wary of:

1. **Overloading the Customer with Information:** Sharing too many details can overwhelm and confuse customers. Focus on the most relevant features.
2. **Using Too Much Jargon:** Technical terms may alienate customers. Always explain features in simple, relatable terms.
3. **Focusing Solely on Features:** Don't just list what the product can do; explain *why* it matters to the customer.

4. **Neglecting Emotional Appeal:** People buy with emotions and justify with logic. Connect emotionally with customers before diving into technicalities.

In-depth product knowledge is not just a tool—it's a weapon. It builds credibility, fosters trust, and empowers sales professionals to present features as tailored solutions. By identifying customer needs, linking features to benefits, and tailoring pitches, salespeople can guide customers seamlessly through the buying journey.

However, product knowledge must be paired with empathy, communication skills, and adaptability. In the next chapter, we'll dive into the art of persuasion and how to influence buying decisions with confidence and integrity.

Chapter 5:

Mastering the Art of Persuasion

Proven Persuasion Techniques for Sales Success

Persuasion is the backbone of effective salesmanship. While some view it as manipulation, ethical persuasion is about guiding customers toward decisions that genuinely benefit them. Mastering persuasion involves understanding human psychology, building trust, and presenting information in a way that resonates with the customer's needs and desires.

1. The Principle of Reciprocity

One of the most effective persuasion techniques is the principle of reciprocity—the idea that people feel obligated to return a favor. In sales, this can be achieved by offering something of value upfront, such as a free product demonstration, a helpful tip, or even a small gift.

For example, offering a free consultation or a sample can create a sense of goodwill, increasing the likelihood that the customer will reciprocate by making a purchase.

2. The Power of Social Proof

People are naturally influenced by the actions and choices of others. Testimonials, case studies, and reviews are powerful tools for building confidence in your product.

A salesperson might say, *"Many of our customers in similar situations found this product extremely helpful. Here's what one of them had to say..."*

3. Scarcity and Urgency

When something is perceived as rare or time-sensitive, its value increases. Limited-time offers, exclusive deals, or low-stock alerts can motivate customers to act quickly.

For example: *"This special offer is only available until the end of the week, and we have just a few units left."*

4. Authority and Expertise

Customers are more likely to trust salespeople who demonstrate authority and expertise. Sharing credentials, experience, or industry knowledge can establish credibility.

For example: *"I've been working with clients in this industry for over a decade, and this solution consistently delivers excellent results."*

5. Consistency and Commitment

People like to remain consistent with their past actions and commitments. Getting a small initial commitment can often lead to a larger one.

For example: *"Would you like me to reserve this product for you while you decide?"*

These techniques, when used ethically and with the customer's best interests in mind, can make the sales process smoother and more productive.

How to Handle Objections Effectively

Objections are a natural part of the sales process. They signal that the customer is engaged but has reservations or concerns. Skilled salespeople see objections not as roadblocks but as opportunities to address concerns and reinforce value.

1. Listen without Interrupting

When a customer raises an objection, resist the urge to interrupt or jump to conclusions. Listen actively and let them fully express their concerns.

For example, if a customer says, *"I'm not sure if this fits my budget,"* respond with empathy: *"I understand; budgeting is always an important consideration. Can you share more about your budget goals?"*

2. Acknowledge and Validate Concerns

Customers want to feel heard and understood. Validating their concerns helps build trust.

For example: *"That's a valid concern, and many customers have felt the same way initially."*

3. Ask Clarifying Questions

Sometimes, objections are vague or surface-level. Asking questions can uncover the root of the concern.

For example: *"Is it the overall cost that concerns you, or are you worried about the payment terms?"*

4. Respond with Value

Address objections by reinforcing the product's value and showing how it aligns with the customer's needs.

For example: *"While the initial cost is an investment, this product will save you money in the long run through reduced maintenance expenses."*

5. Use the Feel-Felt-Found Method

This classic sales technique involves three steps:

- **Feel:** Show empathy (*"I understand how you feel."*)
- **Felt:** Share a relatable experience (*"Other customers have felt the same way at first."*)
- **Found:** Offer reassurance (*"But what they found was that the long-term benefits far outweigh the initial concerns."*)

Handling objections effectively requires patience, empathy, and a problem-solving mindset.

Turning "No" into "Yes" Without Pressure

No salesperson likes hearing the word "no," but it's an inevitable part of the job. However, a skilled salesperson knows that a "no" isn't always final. It's often just a sign that the customer needs more information, reassurance, or time.

1. Understand the Reason Behind the "No"

A flat-out rejection is rare; most "no" responses stem from unresolved concerns. Ask follow-up questions to uncover the reasoning.

For example: *"I understand this might not seem like the right fit at the moment. May I ask what's holding you back?"*

2. Create a Win-Win Scenario

Look for ways to adjust the offer to make it more appealing without resorting to pressure tactics.

For example: *"What if I could offer you a flexible payment plan? Would that make it easier for you?"*

3. Provide a No-Pressure Exit

Sometimes, giving customers space and time can turn a "no" into a "yes." Make it clear they are in control.

For example: *"Take your time to think about it. I'll follow up in a couple of days to see if you have any more questions."*

4. Offer Alternatives

If the original product doesn't fit, suggest alternatives that better align with their needs or budget.

For example: *"I understand this option might not work for you. Let me show you something else that might be a better fit."*

5. Leave the Door Open

Not every sale happens immediately. Ending on a positive note keeps the relationship open for future opportunities.

For example: *"Thank you for your time today. If you ever change your mind, feel free to reach out. I'd be happy to assist."*

The Ethics of Persuasion

While persuasion is an essential sales skill, it must always be applied ethically. Manipulative or high-pressure tactics may yield short-term gains, but they damage long-term relationships and reputations.

Ethical persuasion focuses on:

- Providing accurate and transparent information
- Respecting the customer's autonomy and decisions
- Ensuring the product genuinely meets the customer's needs
- Building relationships rather than just closing sales

Salespeople who prioritize ethics not only foster trust but also build a reputation that attracts repeat business and referrals

Mastering the art of persuasion is a cornerstone of sales success. By understanding proven techniques, handling objections gracefully, and turning "no" into "yes" without pressure, sales professionals can build trust, close more deals, and create satisfied customers.

However, persuasion must always be paired with integrity, empathy, and a genuine desire to help customers. In the next chapter, we'll explore the importance of active listening and how it can transform sales interactions.

Chapter 6:

Closing the Deal with Confidence

Recognizing the Right Moment to Close

In sales, timing is everything. Knowing when to close a deal can make the difference between a successful sale and a missed opportunity. Recognizing the right moment requires keen observation, active listening, and a deep understanding of customer behavior.

1. Buying Signals

Customers often give subtle cues when they are ready to make a purchase. These signals can be verbal or non-verbal:

- **Verbal Signals:** Asking about pricing, payment options, warranties, or delivery timelines.

- **Non-Verbal Signals:** Nodding in agreement, handling the product, or showing excitement.

For example, if a customer asks, *"Is there a warranty included?"* or *"How soon can I have this delivered?"*, they are indicating readiness to close.

2. Trial Closes

A trial close is a technique used to test the customer's readiness without explicitly asking for the sale. Examples include:

- *"Does this product meet your expectations?"*
- *"Would this payment plan work for you?"*

If the customer responds positively, it's time to move toward the final close.

3. Overcoming Indecision

Sometimes, customers hesitate even when they seem ready. Addressing their concerns proactively can nudge them towards a decision.

- *"You seem to really like this option. Is there anything still holding you back?"*

Being attuned to these cues ensures that you don't attempt to close too early (risking pushback) or too late (risking loss of interest).

Techniques for Seamless Deal Closures

Closing techniques are tools every salesperson should master. Different situations call for different approaches, and the best salespeople know when to use each one.

1. The Assumptive Close

This technique assumes the customer has already decided to buy. It works best when strong buying signals are present.

- *"Shall we proceed with the paperwork?"*
- *"Would you like delivery on Monday or Wednesday?"*

2. The Summary Close

Summarize the key benefits and features the customer values most before asking for the sale.

- *"So, to recap: you'll have a 3-year warranty, free delivery, and 24/7 customer support. Are you ready to move forward?"*

3. The Alternative Close

Offer the customer two options, both of which lead to a sale.

- *"Would you prefer the standard package or the premium one?"*
- *"Would you like to pay in full or go with our installment plan?"*

4. The Urgency Close

Create a sense of urgency by highlighting time-sensitive opportunities.

- *"This promotion ends tonight, and I'd hate for you to miss out."*
- *"We only have two units left in stock at this price."*

5. The Emotional Close

Appeal to the customer's emotions and vision for a better future.

- *"Imagine how much easier your life will be with this product."*
- *"Think about the peace of mind you'll have knowing your family is protected."*

6. The Direct Close

Sometimes, the best approach is to be straightforward.

- *"Are you ready to place your order?"*
- *"Let's get the paperwork started, shall we?"*

Handling Last-Minute Buyer Hesitations

Even after the customer seems ready to buy, last-minute hesitations are common. These doubts can stem from fear, uncertainty, or second thoughts. Addressing them confidently is crucial.

1. Identify the Root Cause

Ask questions to uncover the real reason behind the hesitation.

- *"Is there something specific that's making you hesitant?"*
- *"Do you need more time to think it over?"*

2. Revisit Their Needs and Benefits

Remind the customer why they were interested in the product in the first place.

- *"You mentioned earlier that reliability was a top priority, and this product delivers on that promise."*

3. Provide Reassurance

Offer reassurances to calm their concerns.

- *"You're making a great choice, and I'll be here to support you every step of the way."*
- *"Remember, there's a 30-day return policy if you're not fully satisfied."*

4. Use Testimonials and Social Proof

Share success stories or reviews from other satisfied customers.

- *"One of our recent clients had the same concerns, but they've been thrilled with their decision."*

5. Give Them Space (If Needed)

Sometimes, the best approach is to step back and give the customer a little time.

- *"Take a moment to think it over. I'll be right here if you have any questions."*

6. Reinforce the Value Proposition

Remind them of the unique benefits they will gain.

- *"This product isn't just an expense; it's an investment that will pay off over time."*

The Importance of Confidence in Closing

Confidence is the invisible factor that can make or break a sale. Customers can sense uncertainty, and it can make them second-guess their decision.

- **Be Prepared:** Know your product, pricing, and terms inside out.
- **Maintain Eye Contact:** It conveys honesty and assurance.
- **Use Positive Body Language:** Stand tall, smile, and avoid fidgeting.
- **Speak Clearly and Decisively:** Avoid filler words like "um" or "maybe."

A confident salesperson projects competence, and customers are naturally drawn to people who exude certainty.

Learning from Missed Opportunities

Not every deal will close, and that's okay. Each missed opportunity is a chance to learn and grow.

- **Reflect on the Interaction:** What went well? What could have been done differently?
- **Seek Feedback:** If appropriate, ask the customer for feedback.
- **Stay Positive:** One lost sale doesn't define your overall performance.

Sales is a numbers game, and persistence is key.

Closing the deal is both an art and a science. It requires impeccable timing, effective techniques, and the ability to handle last-minute hesitations with grace. Sales professionals who master these skills will not only close more deals but also build lasting relationships with their customers.

In the next chapter, we'll explore how to nurture long-term customer relationships and turn one-time buyers into loyal advocates for your brand.

Chapter 7:

Post-Sale Strategies: Building Lifetime Customers

The Power of Follow-Up and After-Sales Service

Closing a sale is not the end of the customer relationship; it's just the beginning. The follow-up and after-sales service phase is where businesses can solidify trust, ensure customer satisfaction, and lay the groundwork for future transactions.

1. Why Follow-Up Matters

Follow-up is a critical step in building customer loyalty. It shows customers that their satisfaction is a priority, not just their money. Effective follow-up can:

- Reinforce the customer's decision to purchase.

- Provide an opportunity to address any post-purchase concerns.
- Set the stage for upselling or cross-selling additional products or services.

For example, a simple phone call or email a few days after the purchase asking, *"How is everything working out with your new product?"* can leave a lasting positive impression.

2. Providing Exceptional After-Sales Service

After-sales service is about delivering value beyond the initial purchase. This could include:

- Technical support or troubleshooting assistance.
- Easy access to customer service representatives.
- Offering warranties or service plans.

For instance, sending a quick start guide or tutorial video after a product purchase can help customers get the most out of their purchase.

3. Personalized Follow-Up Strategies

Every customer is different, and follow-up efforts should be tailored to individual preferences. Strategies include:

- **Phone Calls:** For high-value clients or significant purchases.
- **Emails:** For regular updates, surveys, or thank-you notes.
- **Personalized Messages:** Handwritten thank-you cards or custom video messages can make customers feel valued.

A good follow-up strategy turns a one-time customer into a repeat client.

Encouraging Repeat Business and Referrals

Repeat customers are often the most profitable customers. They cost less to retain than acquiring new ones and often purchase more over time. Additionally, loyal customers become brand advocates who bring in referrals.

1. Creating Incentives for Repeat Business

Rewarding repeat customers can encourage ongoing loyalty. Effective strategies include:

- **Loyalty Programs:** Points systems, discounts, or exclusive offers for repeat customers.
- **Subscription Models:** Offering convenience through auto-renewals or subscription services.
- **Exclusive Access:** Early access to sales, new products, or VIP events.

For example, *"As a valued customer, enjoy 20% off your next purchase with this exclusive code."*

2. Leveraging Referrals

Satisfied customers are one of the best sources of new business. Encouraging referrals can be as simple as:

- **Referral Bonuses:** Offering discounts or rewards for every successful referral.

- **Social Proof:** Encouraging happy customers to leave reviews or share testimonials.

For example, *"Refer a friend and receive a $50 gift card when they make their first purchase."*

3. Consistent Communication

Stay connected with customers through periodic updates, newsletters, or personalized messages. Share relevant content, upcoming events, or special promotions to keep your brand top-of-mind.

For instance, a monthly newsletter with helpful tips related to the product they purchased can keep customers engaged.

Maintaining Long-Term Customer Relationships

Building lifetime customers isn't just about transactions; it's about building trust, credibility, and emotional connections.

1. Build Trust Through Transparency

Transparency in pricing, policies, and communication builds long-term trust. Customers appreciate honesty, especially when things go wrong.

- Admit mistakes and resolve issues swiftly.
- Be upfront about product limitations or timelines.

For example: *"We apologize for the delay in delivery. Here's an update on your order status."*

2. Provide Continuous Value

Customers are more likely to remain loyal if they feel they're continually receiving value. This can include:

- Educational content like blogs, webinars, or video tutorials.
- Exclusive updates on new features or product improvements.

For instance, a car dealership might offer free annual maintenance checks for loyal customers.

3. Listen and Act on Feedback

Customers want to feel heard. Actively seek feedback through surveys, reviews, or casual conversations. Most importantly, act on that feedback.

- Send follow-up surveys after purchases.
- Address recurring issues proactively.

For example: *"Based on your feedback, we've improved our delivery process to ensure faster shipping."*

4. Celebrate Customer Milestones

Show appreciation for long-term customers by celebrating milestones such as purchase anniversaries, birthdays, or loyalty program achievements.

- Send a thank-you gift.
- Offer a special discount.

For example: *"Happy 1-year anniversary with us! Enjoy 30% off your next purchase."*

5. Build Personal Relationships

Sales isn't just about business; it's about people. Take the time to know your customers on a personal level:

- Remember important details about their preferences.
- Send personalized messages on special occasions.

For example: *"Happy Birthday, Sarah! Here's a little something from us to make your day special."*

Leveraging Technology for Post-Sale Strategies

Modern tools and technology can make post-sale engagement easier and more efficient.

1. CRM Systems

Customer Relationship Management (CRM) software helps track customer interactions, preferences, and purchase history. This allows for:

- Timely follow-ups.
- Personalized communication.

- Better understanding of customer behavior.

2. Automated Email Campaigns

Set up automated email campaigns for follow-ups, anniversaries, or promotions.

- Thank-you emails post-purchase.
- Reminders for scheduled services.

3. Analytics and Data Insights

Use analytics tools to monitor customer engagement and identify opportunities for improvement.

- Track open rates on follow-up emails.
- Analyze feedback survey results.

Common Pitfalls to Avoid in Post-Sale Engagement

1. Neglecting Follow-Up

Failing to follow up after a sale can make customers feel undervalued and forgotten.

2. Overwhelming Customers with Communication

While follow-ups are essential, bombarding customers with emails, calls, or promotions can be counterproductive.

3. Ignoring Negative Feedback

Negative feedback is an opportunity for improvement. Ignoring it can damage your reputation.

Post-sale strategies are not just a nice-to-have—they are a necessity for building a sustainable business. Follow-up and after-sales service reinforce customer satisfaction, while loyalty programs and consistent communication encourage repeat business and referrals.

Maintaining long-term relationships requires trust, value, and genuine care for your customers' needs. By investing in these strategies, businesses can turn one-time buyers into lifelong advocates.

In the next chapter, we'll explore the role of ongoing training and self-improvement for sales professionals to ensure continued growth and success.

Chapter 8:

Sales Lot Etiquette and Professionalism

Best Practices for Sales Professionals

Sales professionals on the sales lot are often the face of the business. Their behavior, attitude, and approach can make or break a sale. Adopting best practices ensures consistency, professionalism, and customer satisfaction.

1. Dress and Presentation

First impressions matter. Sales professionals should present themselves in a manner that reflects credibility and respect for their role.

- Wear clean, professional attire appropriate to the sales environment.
- Maintain good hygiene and grooming.

- Use name tags if they are part of the company uniform.

A polished appearance conveys confidence and attention to detail.

2. Body Language and Communication

Non-verbal cues often communicate more than words.

- Maintain eye contact to show confidence and sincerity.
- Stand or sit with good posture.
- Avoid crossing arms or appearing distracted.

When speaking:

- Use a calm, clear, and friendly tone.
- Listen actively without interrupting.
- Mirror the customer's tone and style to build rapport.

3. Punctuality and Availability

Sales professionals must respect customers' time.

- Arrive on time for scheduled meetings.

- Be prepared with necessary documents, product knowledge, or promotional materials.
- Avoid keeping customers waiting unnecessarily.

4. Know When to Step Back

While enthusiasm is important, overbearing sales tactics can push customers away.

- Give customers space to think.
- Avoid interrupting their conversations or private discussions.
- Be ready to step back while staying accessible.

5. Follow Through on Promises

Trust is built when promises are kept.

- If you promise a callback, make it promptly.
- If you offer a discount or free service, ensure it is honored.
- Always double-check details to prevent errors.

These practices build a strong foundation for customer trust and positive interactions.

The Role of Honesty and Transparency in Sales

In an industry where trust is often a deciding factor, honesty and transparency are non-negotiable.

1. Why Honesty Matters

- Builds long-term relationships.
- Reduces buyer's remorse.
- Enhances brand reputation.

Customers appreciate honesty, especially when dealing with high-value purchases. For example, if a product has limitations, communicating them upfront prevents disappointment later.

2. Be Transparent About Pricing and Policies

Pricing ambiguity often leads to distrust. Sales professionals must:

- Clearly explain pricing structures.
- Disclose any hidden fees.
- Be upfront about return policies and warranties.

For instance: *"This model does have a restocking fee if returned after 30 days. Just wanted to make sure you're aware."*

3. Admit Mistakes

Everyone makes mistakes, but how you handle them matters.

- Own up to errors promptly.
- Offer solutions or compensation where necessary.
- Apologize sincerely.

For example: *"I realize I quoted the wrong price earlier. I apologize for the mistake, and here's the correct figure."*

4. Set Realistic Expectations

Avoid overpromising and underdelivering.

- If a product isn't immediately available, communicate the exact timeline.
- If a feature has limitations, explain them clearly.

When customers feel they can trust your word, they are more likely to return.

Maintaining Professionalism under Pressure

Sales environments are often high-pressure, with tight deadlines, demanding customers, and financial targets. Maintaining professionalism in these situations is a key skill.

1. Stay Calm in Difficult Situations

Angry or frustrated customers are common in sales. Responding with calmness and empathy can defuse tension.

- Listen without interrupting.
- Avoid defensive language.
- Use phrases like *"I understand why you're upset, and I'm here to help resolve this."*

2. Manage Stress Effectively

Sales can be stressful, but professionals must find ways to stay focused.

- Take short breaks when needed.
- Practice stress-relief techniques such as deep breathing.

- Keep perspective and avoid taking rejection personally.

3. Handle Rejection Gracefully

Not every customer will make a purchase, and that's okay.

- Thank them for their time.
- Leave a positive impression.
- Follow up politely if appropriate.

For instance: *"Thank you for considering us. If you ever change your mind, I'll be happy to assist you."*

4. Avoid Office Gossip and Negativity

Professionalism extends to interactions with colleagues.

- Avoid speaking negatively about customers or team members.
- Focus on constructive communication.
- Foster a positive team environment.

5. Seek Support When Needed

It's okay to ask for help.

- If a situation escalates, involve a manager.
- If you lack product knowledge, admit it and seek assistance.

Professional Communication Skills

Strong communication is at the heart of sales professionalism.

1. Active Listening

Truly listen to what the customer is saying.

- Don't interrupt.
- Ask follow-up questions.
- Reflect back on what you've heard.

For example: *"So what I'm hearing is that reliability is your top priority. Is that correct?"*

2. Clear and Concise Language

Avoid jargon or overly complex explanations.

- Keep explanations simple.
- Be direct while remaining polite.

3. Written Communication

Emails, text messages, and follow-up letters should be professional.

- Use proper grammar and spelling.
- Be prompt in your responses.
- Always proofread before sending.

Building a Professional Reputation

Reputation takes time to build but can be destroyed quickly.

1. Consistency is Key

Customers should have the same positive experience every time they interact with you.

2. Go Above and Beyond

Exceed customer expectations whenever possible.

- Follow up proactively.
- Provide personalized service.

3. Keep Learning

Professionalism includes continuous improvement.

- Attend training sessions.
- Learn from feedback.
- Stay updated on product knowledge and industry trends.

Ethical Sales Practices

Ethics are central to professionalism.

1. Avoid Manipulative Tactics

- Don't pressure customers into decisions.
- Avoid misleading statements.

2. Respect Customer Privacy

- Keep personal data confidential.
- Follow all data protection regulations.

3. Be Fair in Negotiations

Negotiate honestly and transparently.

- Avoid favoritism.
- Honor agreed-upon terms.

Leading by Example

Sales professionals set the tone for others.

- Mentor new team members.
- Share best practices.
- Model ethical behavior.

When professionalism is prioritized, it creates a positive culture on the sales lot.

Sales lot etiquette and professionalism are about more than just looking the part—they involve communication, ethical behavior, and the ability to handle pressure gracefully. By following best practices, embracing honesty, and maintaining composure under pressure, sales professionals can build strong relationships with customers and colleagues alike.

In the next chapter, we'll explore how to use data and technology to enhance sales strategies and improve overall performance.

Chapter 9:

Metrics That Matter: Measuring Success on the Sales Lot

Key Performance Indicators (KPIs) for Salespeople

In the fast-paced world of sales, success isn't just about closing deals—it's about measurable performance. Key Performance Indicators (KPIs) are essential tools for evaluating sales performance, identifying strengths and weaknesses, and driving improvement.

1. Sales Revenue

The most obvious KPI is total sales revenue.

- Tracks the overall income generated from sales.
- Provides insights into the salesperson's ability to close high-value deals.

For example: *"Salesperson A generated $200,000 in sales revenue this quarter, exceeding the target by 15%."*

2. Conversion Rate

Conversion rate measures the percentage of leads or prospects converted into actual customers.

- Highlights efficiency in moving customers through the sales funnel.
- A low conversion rate may indicate issues with the sales pitch or follow-up processes.

For example: *"Out of 50 leads, Salesperson B closed 10 deals, resulting in a 20% conversion rate."*

3. Average Deal Size

This KPI measures the average monetary value of each sale.

- Helps identify trends in customer spending.
- Allows salespeople to focus on higher-value opportunities.

For example: *"The average deal size for Salesperson C is $5,000, which is above the team average of $4,200."*

4. Sales Cycle Length

Sales cycle length measures the average time taken to close a deal from the first contact.

- Shorter cycles are often more efficient.
- Longer cycles may indicate challenges in overcoming objections.

For example: *"Salesperson D's average sales cycle is 30 days, compared to the team average of 45 days."*

5. Customer Retention Rate

Repeat customers are essential for sustained success.

- Tracks how many customers return for additional purchases.
- Indicates customer satisfaction and loyalty.

For example: *"Salesperson E maintains a 75% customer retention rate, reflecting strong relationship management skills."*

6. Lead Response Time

The speed of responding to leads can impact conversion rates.

- Faster response times often lead to higher closing rates.

For example: *"Salesperson F responds to leads within an average of 2 hours, compared to the team average of 5 hours."*

Setting Realistic Goals and Tracking Progress

Goals provide direction and purpose. However, setting unrealistic or vague goals can lead to frustration and burnout.

1. SMART Goals Framework

Goals should follow the SMART criteria:

- **Specific:** Clearly defined objectives.
- **Measurable:** Quantifiable targets.
- **Achievable:** Realistic based on resources.

- **Relevant:** Aligned with business objectives.
- **Time-bound:** Deadlines for accountability.

For example: *"Increase monthly sales revenue by 10% over the next quarter."*

2. Breaking Down Larger Goals

Large goals can feel overwhelming. Breaking them into smaller, actionable tasks creates clarity.

- Daily and weekly sales targets.
- Focus on incremental achievements.

For example: *"Make 15 follow-up calls per week to nurture existing leads."*

3. Regular Performance Reviews

Periodic reviews help monitor progress and make adjustments.

- Weekly check-ins with managers.
- Monthly performance assessments.

For example: *"At the end of each month, compare actual sales numbers with projected targets."*

4. Use Technology for Tracking

Sales software and CRM tools simplify goal tracking.

- Automated performance dashboards.
- Real-time analytics and reporting.

For example: *"The CRM dashboard shows Salesperson G is at 85% of their quarterly target."*

Continuous Improvement Strategies

Improvement isn't a one-time activity—it's an ongoing process. Continuous improvement ensures salespeople remain adaptable and effective.

1. Identify Strengths and Weaknesses

Self-assessment and feedback are crucial for growth.

- Conduct performance audits.

- Analyze individual KPIs.

For example: *"Salesperson H excels at lead conversion but struggles with upselling."*

2. Ongoing Training and Development

Sales techniques and customer behaviors evolve.

- Attend sales workshops and seminars.
- Participate in mentorship programs.
- Stay updated on product knowledge.

For example: *"Salesperson I attended a negotiation skills workshop and improved closing rates by 20%."*

3. Role-Playing Scenarios

Practice makes perfect.

- Role-play common sales scenarios.
- Practice objection handling.

For example: *"During role-play sessions, Salesperson J practiced addressing price objections confidently."*

4. Seek and Act on Feedback

Feedback from customers and managers offers valuable insights.

- Conduct post-sale surveys.
- Hold regular one-on-one coaching sessions.

For example: *"Customer feedback highlighted a need for better product demos, prompting targeted training."*

5. Embrace a Growth Mindset

Sales professionals must view challenges as opportunities for growth.

- Stay positive during setbacks.
- Celebrate small wins.

For example: *"After a difficult month, Salesperson K focused on improving follow-up techniques and bounced back with stronger results."*

Leveraging Technology for Sales Metrics

Technology plays a critical role in tracking and analyzing sales performance.

1. CRM Systems

Customer Relationship Management (CRM) tools offer powerful insights.

- Track lead progression.
- Monitor communication history.

For example: *"The CRM system highlighted a drop in follow-ups, allowing the team to address the issue."*

2. Sales Dashboards

Real-time dashboards provide instant performance updates.

- Visualize key metrics.
- Identify trends and patterns.

For example: *"The dashboard revealed a spike in conversion rates after implementing a new follow-up process."*

3. Automation Tools

Automating routine tasks saves time.

- Schedule follow-up emails.
- Generate performance reports.

For example: *"Automated reminders ensured no lead was left unattended."*

4. Data Analytics Platforms

Advanced analytics tools offer deeper insights.

- Predict customer behavior.
- Identify growth opportunities.

For example: *"Data analytics showed that weekday evenings had higher sales conversion rates."*

Avoiding Common Pitfalls in Sales Metrics

1. Focusing Solely on Revenue

While revenue is important, other KPIs like customer satisfaction and retention are equally vital.

2. Ignoring Customer Feedback

Customer insights often reveal valuable improvement areas.

3. Setting Unrealistic Goals

Overly ambitious targets can demotivate the team.

4. Neglecting Follow-Up Actions

Metrics are meaningless without actionable follow-up strategies.

Sales metrics are more than just numbers—they tell the story of performance, highlight growth opportunities, and guide strategic decisions. By focusing on key KPIs, setting realistic goals, and embracing continuous improvement, sales professionals can achieve sustainable success on the sales lot.

In the final chapter, we'll discuss cultivating a winning sales culture and fostering teamwork to ensure long-term success.

Chapter 10:

The Future of Sales Lots: Adapting to Change

How Technology is Transforming Sales Lots

Technology is reshaping every aspect of sales, and sales lots are no exception. From digital tools to data-driven strategies, sales professionals must embrace innovation to remain relevant.

1. Digital Customer Relationship Management (CRM) Systems

CRMs have become essential tools for managing customer data and tracking interactions.

- Store customer preferences and history.
- Automate follow-ups and reminders.
- Provide insights into customer behavior.

For example: *"Salesperson A uses a CRM to track follow-ups, resulting in a 25% increase in customer retention."*

2. Virtual and Augmented Reality (VR & AR)

These technologies are revolutionizing product demonstrations.

- Virtual tours allow customers to explore products remotely.
- AR tools enable interactive product visualizations.

For example: *"Using AR, customers can visualize how a vehicle looks in different colors and trims before purchasing."*

3. AI-Powered Sales Tools

Artificial Intelligence (AI) analyzes data to predict customer behavior and suggest sales strategies.

- Automates repetitive tasks like scheduling and follow-ups.
- Provides data-driven recommendations for upselling.

For example: *"AI tools identified patterns in customer data, boosting sales conversions by 15%."*

4. Online Sales Platforms

E-commerce platforms are complementing traditional sales lots.

- Customers can browse products online before visiting the lot.
- Digital payment options streamline transactions.

For example: *"50% of customers now pre-select their vehicles online before visiting the lot."*

5. Data Analytics and Insights

Data analytics tools provide actionable insights.

- Identify high-performing sales strategies.
- Analyze customer demographics and preferences.

For example: *"Data analytics revealed peak customer footfall occurs on weekends, leading to adjusted staffing schedules."*

Staying Competitive in an Evolving Sales Landscape

The sales industry is dynamic, and sales professionals must adapt quickly to remain competitive.

1. Embracing Omnichannel Sales Strategies

Customers expect seamless experiences across multiple platforms.

- Integrate in-person, online, and mobile sales experiences.
- Provide consistent messaging across all channels.

For example: *"Customers who interacted with both online and offline channels were 30% more likely to make a purchase."*

2. Personalized Customer Experiences

Customers value tailored interactions.

- Use CRM data to personalize communication.
- Offer customized product recommendations.

For example: *"Personalized follow-up emails resulted in higher engagement rates."*

3. Upskilling and Training Sales Teams

Continuous training ensures teams are equipped with modern sales techniques.

- Provide regular workshops.
- Invest in technology training programs.

For example: *"Sales team members trained in digital tools outperformed their peers by 20%."*

4. Sustainability and Ethical Practices

Consumers are increasingly prioritizing ethical businesses.

- Adopt sustainable business practices.
- Communicate transparency and corporate responsibility.

For example: *"Sales lots with sustainable practices reported higher customer loyalty."*

5. Building a Strong Online Presence

A robust digital presence is essential for credibility.

- Maintain active social media accounts.
- Encourage positive online reviews.

For example: *"Sales lots with active social media profiles saw a 40% increase in customer inquiries."*

Preparing for the Next Generation of Sales Professionals

As technology and customer expectations evolve, the next generation of sales professionals must be equipped with the right skills and mindset.

1. Digital Literacy

Sales professionals must be comfortable using technology.

- Familiarity with CRM tools.
- Proficiency in digital communication platforms.

For example: *"Sales trainees with digital proficiency adapted faster to CRM tools."*

2. Emotional Intelligence (EQ)

Emotional intelligence is crucial for building customer relationships.

- Practice active listening.
- Develop empathy and conflict-resolution skills.

For example: *"Salespeople with higher EQ scores demonstrated better customer retention."*

3. Adaptability and Resilience

The sales environment is fast-changing, requiring adaptability.

- Embrace new tools and strategies.
- Stay positive during setbacks.

For example: *"Resilient salespeople outperformed peers during market downturns."*

4. Collaboration and Teamwork

Sales success often depends on teamwork.

- Share knowledge and insights within the team.
- Collaborate across departments.

For example: *"Sales teams that held regular strategy meetings closed more deals."*

5. Ethical Sales Practices

The next generation must prioritize integrity and transparency.

- Build trust with honest communication.
- Avoid aggressive sales tactics.

For example: *"Salespeople focused on honesty achieved higher long-term customer satisfaction."*

Emerging Trends in Sales Lots

1. Hybrid Sales Models

Combining online and in-person sales offers flexibility.

- Virtual consultations paired with on-lot visits.
- Digital paperwork reduces transaction times.

2. Subscription-Based Models

Subscription services for products are gaining traction.

- Customers can pay monthly instead of upfront.
- Creates long-term revenue streams.

3. Automation and Self-Service Kiosks

Self-service kiosks streamline the buying process.

- Customers can browse options independently.
- Reduces reliance on sales staff for routine tasks.

4. Enhanced Customer Insights Through AI

AI tools are refining customer targeting and engagement.

- Predict future buying trends.
- Customize sales strategies for individual customers.

Challenges in Adapting to Change

1. Resistance to Technology Adoption

Some sales teams may resist change.

- Provide ongoing training.
- Highlight the benefits of new tools.

2. Balancing Technology and Human Interaction

Technology should enhance, not replace, human connection.

- Use tools to streamline processes.
- Maintain personal rapport with customers.

3. Data Privacy and Security

With increased reliance on digital tools, data security is crucial.

- Adhere to data protection regulations.
- Educate staff on cybersecurity best practices.

4. Keeping Up with Rapid Changes

Technology evolves quickly.

- Regularly update systems and processes.
- Stay informed about industry trends.

The Road Ahead

The future of sales lots will be shaped by innovation, adaptability, and customer-centric strategies.

1. Focus on Customer Experience

Customer satisfaction will remain central.

- Prioritize seamless and personalized interactions.

2. Leverage Real-Time Data

Instant data insights will guide decisions.

- Monitor performance metrics in real time.

3. Build Agile Sales Teams

Sales teams must remain flexible.

- Encourage a culture of continuous improvement.

4. Invest in Sustainable Practices

Sustainability will become a key differentiator.

- Adopt eco-friendly initiatives.

The sales lot of the future will be defined by technology, customer-centric strategies, and adaptable sales professionals. Staying competitive requires embracing change, investing in continuous improvement, and preparing for the evolving landscape. By doing so, sales professionals can not only survive but thrive in the ever-changing world of sales.

Conclusion

The modern sales lot is no longer just a space where transactions occur—it has become a dynamic environment where relationships are built, trust is earned, and long-term loyalty is cultivated. This book has explored the key elements that contribute to success in this ever-changing landscape, from understanding buyer psychology and mastering the art of persuasion to leveraging technology and data analytics for smarter decision-making.

In the early chapters, we examined the foundational principles of effective salesmanship, including creating positive first impressions, building trust, and tailoring product pitches to customer needs. These timeless skills remain at the heart of every successful sales professional's toolkit.

As the book progressed, we explored advanced strategies for closing deals with confidence, maintaining professionalism under pressure, and developing post-sale relationships to ensure repeat business and referrals. The importance of follow-up, transparency, and honesty cannot be overstated in today's competitive marketplace.

We also addressed the critical role of technology and innovation in shaping the sales lot of the future. Tools such as AI, CRM systems, and data analytics are revolutionizing how sales professionals interact with customers, track performance, and streamline operations. Embracing these tools is no longer optional but a necessity for those who want to stay ahead.

Furthermore, the chapters emphasized the importance of measurable outcomes. Key performance indicators (KPIs) and continuous improvement strategies provide a clear roadmap for tracking success, identifying weaknesses, and making informed adjustments. Success on the sales lot is not just about individual talent but about teamwork, consistency, and a culture of growth.

As we look to the future, it's clear that adaptability will remain a cornerstone of success. Sales professionals must be prepared to evolve alongside emerging trends, whether that means adopting hybrid sales models, exploring subscription-based approaches, or prioritizing sustainability and ethical practices.

The future belongs to sales professionals who can combine timeless principles with innovative techniques. It belongs to those who see every customer interaction not just as an opportunity for a sale, but as the beginning of a long-term relationship.

In closing, success on the sales lot is not defined by luck or chance—it's the result of preparation, strategy, and a deep understanding of both products and people. By embracing the insights and strategies outlined in this book, you're not just preparing to meet sales targets—you're positioning yourself to exceed them, build a reputation for excellence, and create a lasting impact in the world of sales.

The sales lot of tomorrow is already here. Are you ready to step into it with confidence and vision?

www.ingramcontent.com/pod-product-compliance
Lightning Source LLC
Chambersburg PA
CBHW071101240526
45471CB00016B/2286